My Grief Journey

Coloring Book and Journal
(for Grieving Parents)

Author - Laura Diehl

Illustrated by - Kath Brinkman

My Grief Journey: Coloring Book and Journal (for Grieving Parents)

Copyright © 2016 Laura Diehl

Published by Crown of Glory Publishers
PO Box 264
Janesville, WI 53547-0264

TABLE OF CONTENTS

INTRODUCTION

My Grief Journey: Coloring Book and Journal is for those who are learning how to live after the death of their child. We don't know the details of what led you to this journey and the need to work through your grief. But one thing we do know is that you have suffered a very deep loss, and for that we are truly sorry.

This book is different from all the other coloring books out there. First, it is hand drawn. You may see uneven, wobbly lines and maybe even an occasional mistake. This mirrors life much clearer than a perfect computer generated drawing. Life throws things at us that make us feel uneven and wobbly. And occasionally we blow it. But if we continue on, in the end, it will be beautiful. Secondly, *My Grief Journey* is not just a coloring book. It is a guided journey through grief. As you work through the pages, we pray you find hope and healing. Meditate and pray over the words as you color, and be open to what God will do in you.

How to use this book:

Each page has a word to think about, explore, and journal. There is a writing prompt to get you started. Feel free to journal on the lines, throughout the drawings, in the margins, on the written pages or on the back of the picture. So what if it looks messy? That is actually a good representation of where we are in life for the moment, right?

Also, you don't need to go through the pages in order, unless you want to. You might want to jump around to the word that hits what you are feeling at the moment. It's your journey. It's your book. Do it however you want.

Our hope and prayer is that as you work through this journal and color these pages, you may find some measure of healing. Write, vent, color, release, meditate and see what this journey brings.

May you find peace as you invest in the time to grieve your loss, and may He lead you to everlasting peace and joy.

From two who have been touched by grief and seen God do amazing things.

Laura and Kath

A final note:

Some of the things you will be reading are quotes from Laura's books. These portions are italicized, and the name of the book is in parenthesis after the quote, indicating which book the quote has been taken from.

Also, there is a private Facebook community for those who have purchased My Grief Journey to be able to share their pictures and thoughts with each other. If you would like to request access to this page, go to

www.crownofgloryministries.org/gpshope-mgj-facebook/

As soon as you provide your name and email address, you will be given instructions on how to join the group.

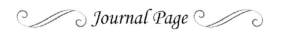

SHOCK

The shock of finding out...the shock of finding yourself in the front row of your child's funeral...the shock of visiting him or her at the cemetery (or having your child handed to you in an urn)...

And just when you are trying to convince yourself it is just a nightmare, something jolts you to reality and brings that shock again.

No one expects to have their child leave this earth ahead of them. It is just so very wrong!

Don't panic. I'm with you. There's no need to fear for I'm your God. I'll give you strength. I'll help you. I'll hold you steady, keep a firm grip on you. (Isaiah 41:10 MSG)

SHOCK

I still think about:

Journal Page

NUMB

How can I feel so much pain and yet at the same time feel nothing?

I am watching life happen around me. I can see it all. I can hear it all. But nothing seems real. It is like I am watching a movie unfold in front of me. Somehow, I know this is a movie of my life, and yet I am also so far removed from it. I am functioning, and yet I am frozen.

I don't like being numb, but it is better than having to face the reality that my child is really gone, and the unbearable pain that will come with it.

When you go through deep waters, I will be with you. When you go through rivers of difficulty, you will not drown. When you walk through the fire of oppression, you will not be burned up; the flames will not consume you. (Isaiah 43:2 NLT)

NUMB

The questions I keep asking:

Journal Page

CONFUSION

How did this happen? I know God could have stopped this. Why didn't He? Why would He let me go through so much pain? Why would He do this to my child?

There can be even more confusion when there was suffering involved, or a sibling saw what happened. Why would God not step in and spare these children? How can He be a good God, if He allows children to suffer?

All I can say is that He is the only one who can bring true peace to any situation. I have learned to trust Him, through many deep trials in my life, including the death of my daughter. He has never failed to pull me out of the pit and back into His light, life, and love.

God is not a God of confusion but a God of peace. (1 Corinthians 14:33 NCV)

CONFUSION

It's so confusing that...

_____

_____

_____

_____

_____

Journal Page

SHATTERED

For the most part, I was able to take out my work box and stay there, but grief had just shattered my "Becca box" into a million pieces. I tried to sweep my grief into a grief box, but the problem with grief is that it cannot stay in a box! Somehow those shattered pieces find a way into all the other boxes. These pieces tend to appear out of nowhere and not always at convenient times. (Laura's husband, Dave, in When Tragedy Strikes)

...Jesus himself was suddenly standing there among them. "Peace be with you," he said. (Luke 24:36 NLT)

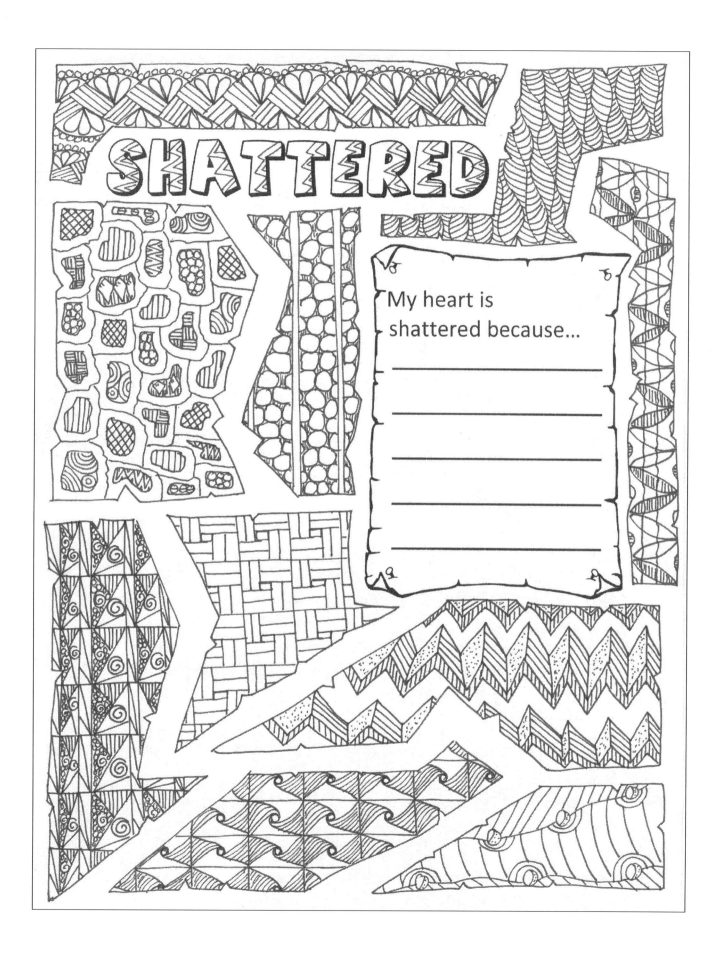

SHATTERED

My heart is
shattered because...

_____

_____

_____

_____

_____

Journal Page

OVERWHELMED

So much to take in. So much to process. So much to do.

It can be hard to get out of bed. It can be hard just to breathe. Has this really happened? Someone please wake me up from this horrible nightmare!

We cannot get through this alone, nor should we try. This is when we need to fall into the arms of God, and let Him carry us.

From the end of the earth I will cry to you whenever my heart is overwhelmed. Place me on the rock that's too high for me. (Psalm 61:2 ISV)

Right now I am
overwhelmed by:

_____

_____

_____

_____

_____

_____

OVERWHELMED

Journal Page

PAREAVOR

What is a pareavor? So glad you asked!

Allow me to share from my book *Come Grieve Through Our Eyes*, which is where the word is first introduced.

As a parent who has experienced this horrific event, I found myself trying to think of a word to describe what I felt, and the only thing that came to me is death—the pain of my own death. A part of us dies along with our child.

This got me thinking. A widow or widower is someone who has lost their spouse; an orphan is someone who has lost their parents. Since it is acknowledged that losing a child is the worst loss a person can go through in life, then why isn't there a word for us?

I have thought and prayed long and hard on this. One day I sat down and listed all the words possible for parents, grief, bereaved, children, etc. to see what I could put together as a word for a grieving or bereaved parent.

That is how I made the word being introduced in this book: PAREAVOR. A pareavor is a parent who has lost a child through death. How did I come up with this?

"Pa" comes from the word parent: a person who is a father or mother; a person who has a child (Merriam-Webster)

"Reave" comes from the word bereave. The meaning of the actual word "reave" (which the word bereave comes from) is: to plunder or rob, to deprive one of, to seize, to carry or tear away (Merriam-Webster).

"Or": indicating a person who does something (Wiktionary)

This sounds like a pretty good description of what happens when a child dies, no matter the age of the child. So a "pareavor" is a parent who has been deprived of their child who was seized and torn away from them through death..

Let the Lord watch over us while we are separated from each other. (Genesis 31:49 NCV)

PAREAVOR

Pareavor is a good word
to describe me because:

_____
_____
_____
_____
_____
_____

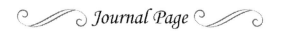

Journal Page

PAIN

Pain is such a generic word, like love. There are so many different kinds, and so many different levels.

The pain of having our child leave this earth goes beyond what can be described. Some pareavors say that time is the only thing that seems to help – lots and lots of time. Some will say that time doesn't take away the pain, but just helps us learn how to manage it.

But we can all agree that we had no idea there is a pain so deep you can forget how to breathe; one that keeps us in a painful confusing fog for days, weeks, months, and even years.

What we suffer now is nothing compared to the glory he will reveal to us later. (Romans 8:18 NLT)

PAIN

I manage my pain by...

Journal Page

REGRET

If only...

If only...

If only...

These thoughts can torment us. At some point we have to let them go, or we will forever be brought to our knees from the bullying pain these thoughts bring. What is done is done. What is gone is gone.

I am pretty sure your child has already forgiven you and released you from all of these things. And when you join him or her, those regrets will be totally wiped away forever. Why wait until then? Release yourself from them right now.

Brothers and sisters, I know that I still have a long way to go. But there is one thing I do: I forget what is in the past and try as hard as I can to reach the goal before me. I keep running hard toward the finish line to get the prize that is mine because God has called me through Christ Jesus to life up there in heaven. (Philippians 3:13-14 ERV)

Journal Page

ANGER

There are a few who don't get angry at God, but most parents who have lost a child through death definitely feel this emotion toward Him. And it's okay. He can take it. Yell at Him; have it out with Him!

Yes, He could have moved His hand and stopped the death of your child and mine. But He didn't do it, for reasons we cannot see or understand.

Most often, our anger at God comes when we think of our loss more than our child's gain; our pain keeps us from trusting that God can see the big picture, and knows something we don't know.

There are others we can be angry with as well, for all kinds of reasons.

It is okay to be angry, and to work through it. But for your own sake, please don't camp out in this place.

Shake with anger and do not sin. When you are on your bed, look into your hearts and be quiet.
(Psalm 4:4 NLV)

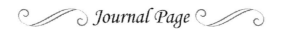# Journal Page

WOUNDED

Losing a child is like an amputation. A part of your very being has been cut off from you. You will never be the same, but you will learn to function again.

When Becca had her amputation as a toddler, it was one of the most traumatic things her little body could go through. There were times when she would feel phantom pains (when the leg that was gone would feel like it was hurting or itching). It took a while for the body and brain to get used to missing that leg. It took time and strength and the will to carry on, but Becca learned to live her life, forever changed, but an amazing life anyway. She had a calling on her life, and losing that leg was not going to stop her.

It can be that way for parents, especially moms, after losing a child. It can be the most horrific thing to go through. It takes time to heal. It takes time to learn how to function without our child. But even though a part of you has died with them, you can live your life again. The effects of that loss will always be there, but God loves you more than you could ever fathom and still has a purpose for you. Just like little Becca, in time you can go on with an amazing life that can touch others. Forever changed by the loss, but also forever changed by the inheritance your child left you. (Laura's husband, Dave, in When Tragedy Strikes)

God, who shows you his kindness and who has called you through Christ Jesus to his eternal glory, will restore you, strengthen you, make you strong, and support you as you suffer for a little while.
(1 Peter 5:10 GW)

I don't feel
the same because...

WOUNDED

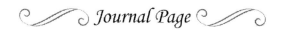

Journal Page

FORGOTTEN

The compassion and concern briefly offered by others comes to an end, and we are left drowning in a sea of grief, not knowing where to go with it for help or support. Not only do we feel alone and forgotten, but even more painful is feeling like our child has been forgotten.

If only those around us knew how much it means to have the life of our child remembered! A card in the mail, a hug, a quick phone call (even if we don't answer and you leave a message) means so much to us. We were thrown into dark and terrifying waters, and ongoing support is a life-line we so desperately need. (Come Grieve Through Our Eyes)

So the Lord answers, "Can a woman forget her own baby and not love the child she bore? Even if a mother should forget her child, I will never forget you... I have written your name on the palms of my hands. (Isaiah 49:15-16 GNT)

FORGOTTEN

I just wish someone would ask:

Journal Page

FEAR

The death of our child can bring so many fears into our lives that we never had before. That is very understandable.

Fear brings torment. God does not give anyone fear. It comes from the enemy of our souls. As those who have faced the unnatural, out-of-order death of our child, we are huge targets for the enemy's fiery darts of fear.

God throws out the fearful torment of the enemy, and replaces it with peace, if we run into His arms and trust in His incredible, deep love for us.

There is no fear in love; but perfect love casts out fear, because fear involves torment. (NKJV) If we are afraid, it ... shows that we are not fully convinced that He really loves us. (1 John 4:19 TLB)

Journal Page

ALONE

We are often torn, because sometimes we find that while we want to be alone, at the same time, we don't want to be lonely.

And it is easy to find ourselves feeling very lonely in a room full of people. Those around us are enjoying conversations, laughing and living a "normal" life, while we are still in a painful fog.

Just being around other people isn't what we are longing for; it is being around people who care, and who will allow us to be whoever we need to be, at any given moment, in our grieving.

This is why pareavors gravitate to each other.

You are not alone. We are here with you.

The Lord is the One Who goes before you. He will be with you. He will be faithful to you and will not leave you alone. (Deuteronomy 31:8 NLV)

ALONE

Is there anyone who understands....

_____
_____
_____
_____

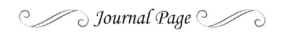

Journal Page

TEARS

I figure if God keeps my tears in a bottle (Psalm 56:8), I must have one of the biggest bottles in heaven! (When Tragedy Strikes)

We cry. We can cry hard, and we can cry often. There are so many tears. And when we think there are no tears left, or we think we are finally past all of the crying, something unexpectedly triggers another round of leaking from our eyes.

It will happen for the rest of our lives – the liquid love spilling from our souls.

You have seen me tossing and turning through the night. You have collected all my tears and preserved them in your bottle! You have recorded everyone in your book. (Psalm 56:8 TLB)

TEARS

I cry when...

Journal Page

ANXIOUS

I used to tell myself I wasn't worried, I was just anxious. But there really isn't much difference, is there? Both of them are being concerned in a negative way about something in the future that we probably don't have much control over.

Both fear and faith come from the same root – our thoughts and emotions about the unknown future. So that means we get to choose. Am I going to be anxious and worry, or am I going to trust that even though the worst possible nightmare has happened in my life, God is still taking care of me and will continue to be the peace in my storms – no, make that the hurricanes – of my life?

Don't fret or worry. Instead of worrying, pray. Let petitions and praises shape your worries into prayers, letting God know your concerns. Before you know it, a sense of God's wholeness, everything coming together for good, will come and settle you down. It's wonderful what happens when Christ displaces worry at the center of your life. (Philippians 4:6-7 MSG)

ANXIOUS

I worry about:

_____

_____

_____

_____

_____

_____

Journal Page

HELPLESS

Being helpless is such a horrible feeling for sure, especially when it comes to our children. And we have faced the ultimate extreme of helplessness; we were not able to protect our child from death. Oh the pain and guilt of being such a bad parent!

Or were we? Neither life nor death is in our hands. God is the one who gives life within the womb. And God chooses when each person takes their last heartbeat. We may cry out, "That's not fair!" May I remind you, many things are not fair in this fallen sinful world, especially from our viewpoint?

Personally, I have made the choice not to feel helpless, but to be hopeful. I am determined to stay connected to God, believing that He is truly good all the time and not just when I get my own way. I believe with every fiber of my being that my daughter is with Him in the safest and most wonderful place possible, and until I join her, I will move forward toward being happy and fulfilled in this life.

And that is how we break the bondage of feeling helpless.

Stay joined to me and I will stay joined to you. No branch can produce fruit alone. It must stay connected to the vine. It is the same with you. You cannot produce fruit alone. You must stay joined to me. I am the vine, and you are the branches. If you stay joined to me, and I to you, you will produce plenty of fruit. But separated from me you won't be able to do anything. If you don't stay joined to me, you will be like a branch that has been thrown out and has dried up. (John 15:4-6 ERV)

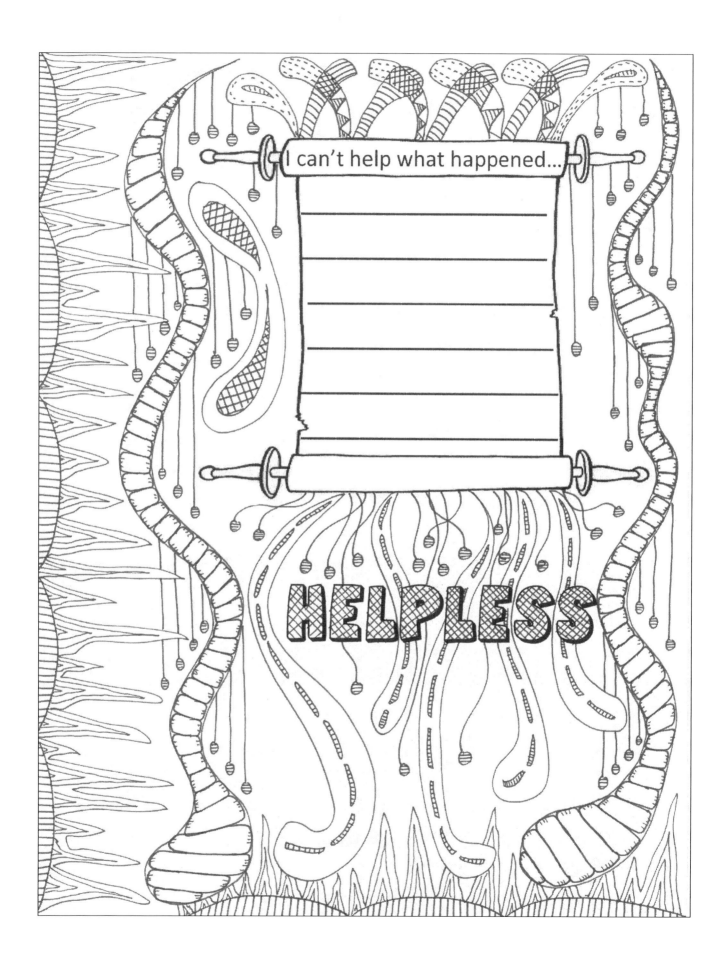

Journal Page

SORROW

Sorrow and suffering. Those two words always seem to be together. And they don't even begin to describe how we feel after the death of our child.

I was having it out with God about this one day. The depth of the pain was unbearable. I knew somehow I had to get past it; that I couldn't go on living this way in such deep darkness and depression. I also knew I had to be the one to allow myself to release it, but didn't know how.

Somewhere I heard or read the words "Spiritual blessings come wrapped in trials." I wrote a note saying: "The loss of a child is an awfully deep trial to wrap a blessing in!" God's unexpected answer followed, "I know, because My Son died, and it was wrapped in the blessing of you!" (When Tragedy Strikes)

God knows deep sorrow, even based on the death of His Son. And within that sorrow, He carried ours as well.

Let your sorrow melt into His sorrow, and you will begin to see to the other side.

He was despised and rejected—a man of sorrows, acquainted with deepest grief. We turned our backs on him and looked the other way. He was despised, and we did not care. Yet it was our weaknesses he carried; it was our sorrows that weighed him down. (Isaiah 53:3-4 NLT)

SORROW

I try to hide my sorrow when:

_____
_____
_____
_____
_____

Journal Page

LONGING

A longing is a strong, persistent desire or craving, an aching, especially for something unattainable or distant. (Taken from dictionary.com.)

We long for our child who has left this earth. We long to hear their laugh, be able to give them a hug, or to hear them say, "I love you."

We are also thankful that this is not "unattainable," but only "distant," as we will see them again someday in a place where there are no more tears, no more pain, and no more separation.

"...having been taken away from you for a short while—in person, not in spirit—were all the more eager with great desire to see your face." (1 Thessalonians 2:17 NASB)

LONGING

I wish.....

_____

_____

_____

_____

_____

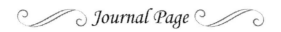

Journal Page

HOPE

When we have no hope, we have no desire to live.

We know the enemy is out to steal from us and kill us. If he can't do it physically, he will do it emotionally. When our child dies, we have the biggest red target on us for the enemy to do exactly that. He steals our hope, leaving us wanting to die to go be with our child. Even if we have other children, a wonderful marriage and had a life full of purpose and passion before our child's death, it all comes crashing down and we are left in a world of darkness and hopelessness.

However, the death of our child did not blindside God like it might have done to us. That means we do not have to stay a slave, chained to our prison of darkness with no hope. Jesus came to break every chain that could ever try to keep us bound. He will carry us through this valley of death, back into a place of abounding hope.

Now may the God of hope fill you with all joy and peace in believing, that you may abound in hope by the power of the Holy Spirit. (Romans 15:13 NKJV)

There is a
possibility that...

HOPE

Journal Page

SURRENDER

During grief, people either move toward God or away from Him. But when we move away from Him, we are moving away from the One who can help us the most. God wants to walk with us through this valley of death. He wants to give us comfort. He wants to give us strength. He wants to give us hope. These are all things we desperately need. But if we choose to move away from Him, we will continue to desperately need these things. This is a time to get as close to God as you possibly can.

As I was writing the last paragraph, I got a picture of a distraught child crying uncontrollably. In the picture, I see a father bending down to pick up that child. The child is so upset he is kicking and screaming and fighting the father, who is trying to pick him up. Eventually the child runs out of strength and relaxes in the embrace of his loving father. And now that child can receive the comfort, strength, and hope he wants and needs. It is the same with us. Don't fight the One who can give you the very things you need. Surrender, let Him embrace you and carry you in His strong arms of love. (When Tragedy Strikes)

Yes, I must find my rest in God. He is the God who gives me hope. (Ps. 62:5 NIRV)

SURRENDER

What I need to let go
of to move forward:

_____

_____

_____

_____

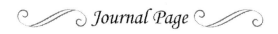

Journal Page

TIME

Time can be terrifying to us now. Time means we are getting further away from our child. I am dreading the day my daughter has been gone for five years, and can't imagine her not being here for ten or twenty years or more. The thought of it can take my breath away and bring stinging tears!

And yet, as time goes by, it also means we are getting closer to seeing our child again, and that makes me so excited!

The pendulum of time...it is all in our perspective.

This body that decays must be changed into a body that cannot decay. This mortal body must be changed into a body that will live forever. When this body that decays is changed into a body that cannot decay, and this mortal body is changed into a body that will live forever, then the teaching of Scripture will come true: "Death is turned into victory!" (1 Corinthians 15:53-54 GW)

Journal Page

FORGIVE

I believe forgiveness is one of the first steps to getting out of this pit, and it is not based on our feelings. It is a choice we make. When it comes to the death of our child, including the circumstances around it and the domino effects it may cause, we can discover we don't have what it takes within ourselves to forgive. But God already knows that, and He has made a way for us to be able to forgive in His strength—a strength far beyond our own.

It won't be a onetime thing but a process; sometimes a very slow and painful process. You will find yourself having to choose forgiveness over and over again. ...Is it extremely difficult? Yes, for sure. Is it impossible? Only if you say so. It truly is your choice to hang onto unforgiveness and be destroyed by bitterness, or to start the process of forgiveness and eventually find freedom. (When Tragedy Strikes)

Then Peter came to him and asked, "Lord, how often should I forgive someone who sins against me? Seven times?"
"No, not seven times," Jesus replied, "but seventy times seven!" (Matthew 18:21-22 NLT)

FORGIVE

I am struggling to forgive because...

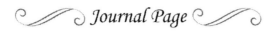

Journal Page

MEMORIES

When our child first dies, the strongest memories are of the death and the circumstances surrounding the death.

When the fun and wonderful memories start to return, it is usually with pain, because we know those memories are all that we have left of our precious child.

Eventually, our hearts begin to smile at the memories, and it even reaches our faces, as we smile at the thought of our child and the joy they brought us.

And from there, we can actually find ourselves grateful for the time on earth we had with our child, no matter how short, instead of angry and bitter for the time we lost.

...for I will turn their mourning into joy, and I will comfort them and make them rejoice, for their captivity with its sorrows will be behind them. (Jeremiah 31:13 TLB)

One memory I want
to hold onto:

MEMORIES

LIFE

Bad things happen to good people. Horrible and evil things happen to God's people. You have paid what many will say is the ultimate price of sacrifice on this earth—the death of your son or daughter. (Sound familiar? I know someone else who paid the price of His Son a little over two thousand years ago.) But you did not give your child willingly, or have a choice.

The question is: Are you going to let it be a wasted sacrifice? Are you going to become bitter or better? What value are you going to place on the life of your child? That is where the mind shift happens. Life or death?

I refuse to let death cause more death! I will NOT give the enemy that kind of a victory! Because Jesus lives, I can live. I have allowed my God to make good on His promises in my life, to give strength to the weary and hope to the hopeless. And I will allow that hope to continue to grow as it becomes joy that reaches beyond death, both my child's and mine. (When Tragedy Strikes)

I came that they may have and enjoy life, and have it in abundance [to the full, till it overflows].
(John 10:10 AMP)

LiFE

I can honor my child's life by:

_____

_____

_____

_____

_____

_____

BELIEVE

I can choose to believe there is no God or He would have saved my child. I can choose to believe that if there is a God, He isn't good and He isn't fair or He would have saved my child. Both of those options leave me feeling angry and empty. I have chosen the third option. There is a God, His thoughts and ways are so much higher than mine, He loves me with a perfect love, and even though I don't understand why He has allowed this to happen, I still trust Him with my life both here on earth and for eternity. This option has brought me to a place of peace, rest, hope, and life again—even within the pain. (When Tragedy Strikes)

If I can believe it, and so many other pareavors can believe it, you can too.

But who could possibly fight and win this battle except by believing that Jesus is truly the Son of God? (1 John 5:5 TLB)

BELIEVE

I believe God will...

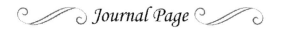

Journal Page

FAMILY

When we have to say a final goodbye to our child, it affects everything. The word "family" takes on a whole new meaning. Our family will never be complete again. There are no replacements for child loss. Ever. And because of that, phrases with the word family in them can bring on crashing emotions.

Any kind of family gathering, event, or even advertisements, is a glaring reminder of the child we are missing.

So many events become bittersweet... (such as another child's wedding, or becoming a grandparent.)

We have to do our best to choose to focus on the blessings we have, and lean into the sweet, instead of the bitter, but it can be extremely difficult. (Come Grieve Through Our Eyes)

He has sent me to the sorrowing (grieving) people... I will give them a crown to replace their ashes. I will give them the oil of gladness to replace their sorrow. I will give them clothes of praise to replace their spirit of sadness. (Isaiah 61:3 ICB)

FAMILY

What "family" means to me now...

_____

_____

_____

_____

Journal Page

RESILIENT

Young children are so very resilient, aren't they? It seems they can bounce back from just about anything. As we get older, it becomes harder to let things go and move forward without wounds and scars.

Don't give up! Don't give up on life. Don't give up on hope. Don't give up on happiness, laughter and joy. I believe your child would be so disappointed to know he or she was the cause of so much pain that you just lived out the rest of your life waiting to die.

There are people who want and need you in their lives. God still has a plan and purpose for you. Fight for it. It is worth it!

The nights of crying your eyes out give way to days of laughter. (Psalm 30:5 MSG)

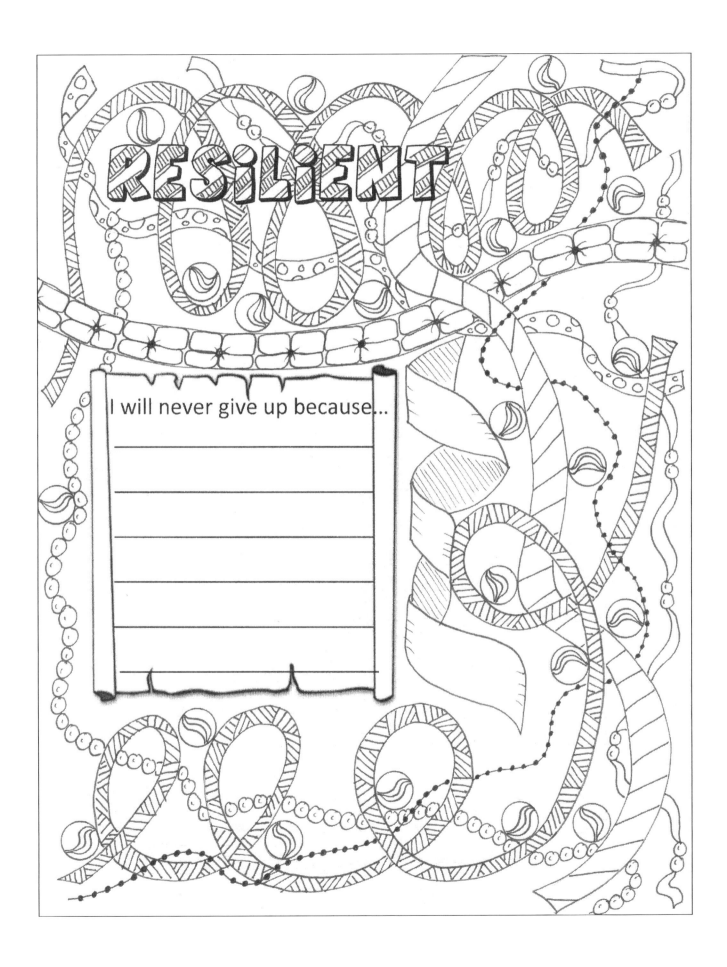

RESiLiENT

I will never give up because...

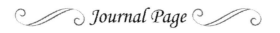

Journal Page

HEAVEN

As a pareavor, I have three things that I think are important about the subject of heaven.

1. Being a spiritual person doesn't automatically remove the painful effects of our child leaving this earth ahead of us. Knowing that our child is in heaven and we will see him or her again someday in glory does not bring a God-sized eraser and take away all the pain.

2. Some parents have a fear of not knowing if their child is in heaven.

   I believe God is big enough to have made every opportunity possible for your child to accept Him before leaving this earth. This could easily have happened during a time you know nothing about (including crying out to Him at the moment of death)...Not having the information you want to have doesn't mean it did not happen at some point in their lives. (When Tragedy Strikes)

3. You are not a terrible person for having a stronger desire to get to heaven to see your child than to see Jesus. You have made an extremely valuable deposit there!

So we do not look at what we can see right now, the troubles all around us, but we look forward to the joys in heaven which we have not yet seen. The troubles will soon be over, but the joys to come will last forever. (2 Corinthians 4:18 TLB)

How I picture my child
in heaven:

HEAVEN

Journal Page

TRUST

Every step on our life journey is actually a step of trust. We either trust in others, in ourselves, or in God. What happens when it is more than a step and we need to take a giant leap of chasms in the dark? What about when we have to scale steep mountains, not knowing what is at the top? And then there is this valley of death we are crossing through. These are the times when trusting completely in others (or ourselves) will eventually fail. Only God knows the difficulty we face, and where the best place is to step, for each part of our life journey. The best thing we can do is take our eyes off the journey and focus on the One who never leaves our side as He helps us through the next step on the path. (When Tragedy Strikes)

Trust in and rely confidently on the Lord with all your heart and do not rely on your own insight or understanding. In all your ways know and acknowledge and recognize Him, and He will make your paths straight and smooth [removing obstacles that block your way]. (Proverbs 3:5-6 AMP)

TRUST

I trust God to take care of...

_____

_____

_____

_____

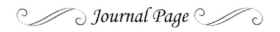

Journal Page

HEALING

When our child leaves this earth, we don't think it is ever possible for our broken heart to heal. Other bereaved parents who have been on this path for a while tell us it will happen, but our pain is so deeply intense, we just can't believe them.

But then it starts to happen. So slowly, we don't even notice it at first.

Time alone does not heal our shattered hearts. It's not time that heals, but what you do in that time. (Come Grieve Through Our Eyes)

There are definitely things that can be done to help the healing process. This book is one of those. Ask God what else will help you. He does not want you to stay wounded and broken. He paid the ultimate price for our healing, both physically and emotionally.

He heals those who have broken hearts. He takes care of their wounds. (Psalm 147:3 NIRV)

I felt a measure of
healing when...

_____

_____

_____

_____

HEALiNG

Journal Page

PEACE

Some people think peace is feeling good about a situation. I have found that peace is resting in God in spite of the situation. It is a belief that God is going to come through and somehow things are going to be okay.

You might be thinking, "How can things possibly be okay when my child has died?" I completely understand. (Remember, I have been there...)

God's peace is beyond what we can understand. Sometimes He speaks peace to the wind and waves, calming the storm surrounding us; other times He holds us through the storm, and speaks peace to the wind and waves raging our hearts.

This is one of those times he wants to speak peace to the storm inside of us.

I have told you all this so that you may have peace in me. Here on earth you will have many trials and sorrows. But take heart, because I have overcome the world. (John 16:33 NLT)

PEACE

I feel at peace about...

Journal Page

COMFORT

When our child first leaves us, there is absolutely nothing that will comfort us. Even if we know in our head that he or she is no longer suffering here on this earth and is in heaven with Jesus, our heart and soul don't care. We just want our child back here with us.

We smell his clothes. We cradle her possessions. We stare at his picture. We sit on her bed. In some strange way, these things bring us comfort, keeping us attached to our child. It's no wonder we take so long to part with their belongings (and some items we will keep until we leave this earth to join our child).

We get a tattoo or a special piece of jewelry we hardly ever take off. We put their picture in the front of our wallet so we can constantly see his or her smiling face.

Comfort...

As you continue on this journey, may you feel God Himself wrap His loving arms around you, giving you comfort in the very deepest parts of your soul.

Even in the unending shadows of death's darkness, I am not overcome by fear. Because You are with me in those dark moments, near with Your protection and guidance, I am comforted. (Psalm 23:4 VOICE)

What still
brings me comfort:

_____

_____

_____

_____

_____

COMFORT

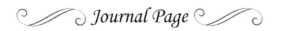

Journal Page

REST

The rest we need to come into is not a time and a place. It is a position. But often we must begin with the time and place in order to learn to live in that position.

That means we have to set time aside specifically to be alone in God's presence. We need to "just be" in the stillness of His presence, where He can speak peace to us and fill us with His extravagant love, especially if we have a hard time believing He truly loves us after not stepping in to save our child from earthly death.

I wish God would just speak a command and make it all better, taking away the pain and replacing it with constant peace and rest, but it hasn't happened that way. Learning how to live in that place has been a process. (When Tragedy Strikes)

I believe learning to rest in God is a must, if you want to get out of your place of darkness.

Come to me, all of you who are tired and have heavy loads, and I will give you rest. Accept my teachings and learn from me, because I am gentle and humble in spirit, and you will find rest for your lives. (Matthew 11:28-29 NCV)

REST

Rest comes to my soul when

_____

_____

_____

_____

_____

Journal Page

GRACE

I cannot overemphasize how important it was for me to make allowances for my family members, especially my wife, in the way they processed their grief. We all handle grief in different ways and on different timelines. My other four children all grieved in different ways and some longer than others. They all still have times when they miss Becca immensely. I encourage all of them to allow each other the space they need to grieve in their own way and not expect the others to grieve in the same way they themselves do.

Laura ... was struggling, even though she knew without a doubt where Becca was and the glory she was experiencing. Was it normal for this to be so hard and go on so long? Truth is, absolutely! Pretty much everything is "normal" when it comes to grief, it seems. (Laura's husband, Dave, in *When Tragedy Strikes*)

Grace, grace, and more grace...

Grow in the loving-favor (grace) that Christ gives you. Learn to know our Lord Jesus Christ better. He is the One Who saves. May He have all the shining-greatness now and forever. Let it be so.
(2 Peter 3:18 NLV)

I can give grace to others by...

_____

_____

_____

_____

GRACE

Journal Page

LIVE

When our child dies, we want to die also. Even if we have other children still here whom we love deeply, it is so difficult to get past death to be able to live again.

As grieving parents, we know we are missing out on life that is continuing on around us, but the fog and pain are so strong it's like we don't care. And yet we do care. So much confusion...so much pain...too much to think about through our fog.

We will never be the same person we were before our tragic event, the death of our child. We have to find within ourselves the strength to make a choice... Do I choose to allow my soul to die and live the rest of my life in my shell of a body? (From Ring Bearer to Pallbearer)

There are those who choose to fight their way out, and those who don't. There are those who choose to die emotionally, and those who choose to find a way to live.

We pray you make the choice to live.

I didn't die. I lived! ...Swing wide the city gates—the righteous gates! I'll walk right through and thank God! This Temple Gate belongs to God, so the victors can enter and praise. (Psalm 118:17-20 MSG)

LIVE

What I still have to live for:

Journal Page

THRIVE

I know that my life will never be the same, but I could not come into agreement that it would always be dark and not worth living. I have four other children and grandchildren. I have a calling on my life and an international ministry. I have the Seed of Hope and Life living inside of me. As horrific as it was, I did not believe the death of my child was where God reached His limit, and He was unable to help me work through it in triumph to a victorious life. (When Tragedy Strikes)

Our daughter Becca had an amputation at three years old. But she did not live her life in survival mode, she thrived. Yes, there were times of pain, frustration, and tears. But that was not the normal way of life for her. She had a tenacity that if any of her friends could do something, she could do it, too. And she did.

We live in survival mode for a long time. But eventually we begin to "wake up" in our souls. We become weary of the lifeless shell we have become. God has created us all with a desire to not just survive, but to thrive. Go for it!

God can do anything, you know—far more than you could ever imagine or guess or request in your wildest dreams! He does it not by pushing us around but by working within us, his Spirit deeply and gently within us. (Ephesians 3:20 MSG)

THRiVE

What can I do to
thrive instead of just survive?

_____

_____

_____

_____

Journal Page

JOY

I am not about to tell you that losing your child will turn into something joyous in your life. But I will tell you it is possible to have joy again in your life, beyond the grief. (When Tragedy Strikes)

That joy is not based on outward circumstances which can go away if those circumstances change, nor is it some euphoric happiness. It is based on a constant inner knowing of Truth, beyond the outward circumstances. It is an undercurrent of contentment, confidence and that seed of hope that has been planted, and is now growing and bearing fruit in my life.

When I said, "My foot is slipping," your unfailing love, LORD, supported me. When anxiety was great within me, your consolation brought me joy. (Psalm 94:18-19 NIV)

JOY

I am hopeful joy will come again because...

Journal Page

FUTURE

The death of our child did not blindside God. In His eyes, we still have a life to live. He has a plan for us, and believe it or not, it is a good plan. Does it seem next to impossible to believe that? How can a good plan for our future be one that is without our child in it?

I had to learn the reality of the truth that my plans are not God's plans. His ways are not my ways. His thoughts are not my thoughts. I have grown into a deeper faith in how awesomely powerful my God is. That He really can take something as horrific as the death of a child, and somehow, miraculously, bring good from it.

If my focus is on my loss, I cannot rise above it to face my future. But if my focus is on my promised future, then it is much easier to rise above the loss and step forward into that future and the good things God still has for me. Let's focus on our promised future...

For I know the plans I have for you," says the Eternal, "plans for peace, not evil, to give you a future and hope—never forget that. (Jeremiah 29:11 VOICE)

I can still look forward to the future because:

_____

_____

_____

_____

FUTURE

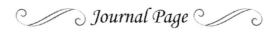# Journal Page

LAUGHTER

How can we possibly smile, or ever be happy again after our child dies? Just the thought of it can make us feel guilty.

But we can, and not only that, it is exactly what we need to do. And we need to reintroduce fun and laughter into our lives, because laughter is medicine to the soul.

If it was reversed (like we all wish it was) would you want your child to remain isolated, depressed and hopeless, believing that life was not worth living without you? Of course not! When we stop and think about it, most of us know in our hearts that our child would not want us to live our lives out that way either.

It's okay to have hope. It's okay to smile. It's okay to laugh and enjoy life again. From one pareavor to another, I give you permission.

A happy heart is good medicine and a joyful mind causes healing, but a broken spirit dries up the bones.
(Proverbs 17:22 AMP)

LAUGHTER

It is okay to laugh again because...

_____

_____

_____

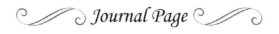

Journal Page

PURPOSE

Each of us has a set number of days here on this old earth, and then we move on to the glorious side of eternity. Our child's time here was much too short as far as we are concerned, and we were supposed to go first. But the fact remains, our child has now moved on to his or her permanent home, and is more alive and full of life than we are! For reasons we don't understand, their purpose on earth was completed, before ours was.

So now it is important that we continue moving forward in our earthly purpose, so that when we join our child who is waiting for us, we will both hear the wonderful words, "Well done, good and faithful servant...Enter into the joy of your Lord." *(Matthew 25:21 NKJV)*

We can only keep on going, after all, by the power of God, who first saved us and then called us to this holy work. We had nothing to do with it. It was all His idea, a gift prepared for us in Jesus long before we knew anything about it. But we know it now. Since the appearance of our Savior, nothing could be plainer: death defeated, life vindicated in a steady blaze of light, all through the work of Jesus.
(2 Timothy 1:9 MSG)

How can I use this experience to help others?

PURPOSE

Journal Page

THANKFUL

One of the most powerful keys you have that will unlock yourself from the chains of death, is to be thankful.

This is something we choose to do, not based on our emotions or how we feel, but based on the truth of who God is.

Start with the smallest things. If you do it consciously and consistently, you will find a spark of hope igniting. Keep going, and it will turn into light and life.

Even if you don't feel it, you can speak your words of thanks to a God who made sure this wasn't the end, but just a transfer into the beginning of something so wonderful it cannot even be fully described!

But let me tell you something wonderful, a mystery I'll probably never fully understand...In the resurrection scheme of things, this has to happen: everything perishable taken off the shelves and replaced by the imperishable, this mortal replaced by the immortal. Then the saying will come true: death swallowed by triumphant Life! Who got the last word, oh, death? Oh, death, who's afraid of you now? It was sin that made death so frightening and law-code guilt that gave sin its leverage, its destructive power. But now in a single victorious stroke of Life, all three—sin, guilt, death—are gone, the gift of our Master, Jesus Christ. THANK GOD! (1 Corinthians 15:56-58 MSG)

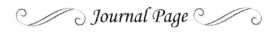

Journal Page

JOURNEY

Our life here on earth is not a destination, it is a journey.

When we are going on a trip, sometimes we make plans, knowing exactly where we are going, and get there without any problems. Sometimes we know where we want to go, but need a map or a GPS to guide us to the right place. And sometimes the road changes and even the GPS has no idea where we are!

That is how we feel after the death of our child. But the good news is, if we keep going, we will eventually either figure out where we are, to be able to get back on our journey, or we will find someone who knows the area who can help us navigate back to road we need to be on.

I hope and pray this book is a useful navigation tool, to get you back onto the journey of life God has for you. Let's go forward together!

I'm not saying that I have this all together, that I have it made. But I am well on my way, reaching out for Christ, who has so wondrously reached out for me. Friends, don't get me wrong: By no means do I count myself an expert in all of this, but I've got my eye on the goal, where God is beckoning us onward—to Jesus. I'm off and running, and I'm not turning back. (Philippians 3:12 MSG)

What I have learned
on this journey:

_____
_____
_____
_____

JOURNEY

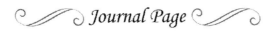

Journal Page

ABOUT THE AUTHOR

Laura Diehl, along with her husband, Dave, are the founders of GPS Hope (Grieving Parents Sharing Hope) which extends hope and healing to all grieving parents through a growing list of resources and a loving community to encourage one another in their unique, difficult journey. This ministry was started after the death of their oldest daughter, Becca. (You can read Laura's story about Becca at www.gpshope.org.)

In 2008, Laura also founded Crown of Glory Ministries. This is a multi-faceted ministry to encourage and equip all ages of the Body of Christ who desire a deeper Kingdom life, by helping them transform their vision, their authority, and their identity. (See the Crown...Wear the Crown... Be the Crown.)

"Kidz Korner" is a monthly article published for Impact Ministries International, written by Laura for children. It is based on several decades of children's ministry experience, encouraging kids to go deeper in their relationship with the Holy Spirit.

Dave and Laura live in Southern Wisconsin, and Laura loves to travel, which is good because she has traveled as an ordained minister for many years both nationally and internationally.

Laura is available as an author, speaker, minister and teacher, and can be contacted by email at laura@crownofgloryministries.org.

ABOUT THE ILLUSTRATOR

Kath Brinkman has been a longtime friend of Laura Diehl. They were actually roommates (along with Becca as a young toddler) and did many double dates with the men who became their husbands, and were in each other's weddings. Kath was the friend Laura leaned on the most when Becca died, and Laura was one of the first people Kath reached out to when her son-in-law Jerod was believed to be dead, as several fire departments came together to search for him (buried in a grain bin at the ethanol plant where he worked).

Kath's teaching profession started as a Kindergarten teacher. She stepped down to homeschool her four children for fourteen years, and for the last eleven years has been a high school teacher at a local private Christian school. Kath has also had the opportunity to be a summer school teacher in the public school system for thirty years.

She has a gift for teaching any age. This gift has been a blessing to the Body of Christ in many ways, including running the drama team as a youth leader, directing VBS, teaching Sunday school for various groups and ages, teaching Bible studies, and leading women's ministry. Her passion is working with and ministering to both teens and women.

Kath loves to read, go on long bike rides, art journal, and draw.

She has a strong calling on her life to bring release to the captives, as God often uses her life circumstances to minister to the hurting and those in chains.

ABOUT GPS HOPE
(GRIEVING PARENTS SHARING HOPE)

GPS Hope is a place for those who are going through the deep dark blackness of losing a child, to find encouragement and strength. It is a safe place for the shattered hearts of pareavors to take off their masks and be allowed to grieve as needed.

When Dave and Laura became pareavors, they didn't know anyone who had lost a child, could not find any local support groups for parents who were grieving the loss of a child (a different kind of grief than any other) and were left trying to navigate through the suffocating grief on their own.

Many books Laura read left her remaining in the place of hopelessness and despair, and seemed to indicate it was a land of no return. That just wasn't acceptable to her. There had to be a way to stop the intense stabbing pain that left one unable to function for months and years; a way to move forward, not just as a shell of a person waiting to die, but a survivor with something to give, and a full life to live.

There had to be a way to honor their daughter with life, not more death.

Their faith in God and belief in His ability to give them that life, pulled Dave and Laura out of that deep black pit that pareavors know all too well. That same faith in God has led them to where they are now, and where they continue to walk, one day at a time. They have learned to persevere and push past the tragic event, going beyond hope, to a place with fullness of purpose and meaning.

GPS Hope was birthed because Dave and Laura Diehl believe this is possible for *all* pareavors. It exists to give direction to hope, healing, and light, by offering various "tools" and resources to this unique group of parents.

RESOURCES

Website: www.gpshope.org
On the GPS Hope website, you will find the following
- Dates and information for occasional GPS Hope events (get-away retreats, etc.)
- A store to purchase Laura's books and other items
- A free Members Library, including the following items
  - *From Ring Bearer to Pallbearer: Giving a Voice to Bereaved Siblings and Grandparents* (available exclusively from GPS Hope)
  - 36 scriptures of Hope
  - A Prayer for Pareavors
  - Eight Things to Avoid Saying to a Grieving Parent
  - Ten Ways to Honor the Life of Your Child
  - Joy Verses

GPS Hope Facebook page: **www.facebook.com/groups/GPSHope**
Laura Diehl Author Facebook page: **www.facebook.com/lauradiehlauthor**
YouTube Channel: **Laura Diehl** (every Friday a short video is posted)

Crown of Glory Ministries website: **www.crownofgloryministries.org**
Crown of Glory Ministries Facebook page: **www.facebook.com/crownofgloryministries.laura**

NOTE: There is a **private Facebook community for those who have purchased** *My Grief Journey* to be able to share their pictures and thoughts with each other. If you would like to request access to this page, go to

www.crownofgloryministries.org/gpshope-mgj-facebook/

As soon as you provide your name and email address, you will be given instructions on how to join the group.

OTHER BOOKS BY LAURA DIEHL

When Tragedy Strikes: Rebuilding Your Life With Hope and Healing After the Death of Your Child

As a grieving parent, there can be a feeling of desperation to find someone farther ahead on the path who can understand the crushing pain that makes you feel like you can't even breathe at times. Laura Diehl was plunged into that place of darkness with the death of her daughter, and meets the deep need to connect with others who have experienced what cannot be put into words. *When Tragedy Strikes* is the raw account of her journey from deep darkness back into light and life, extending a hand of hope to those traveling on the path behind her, who need to rebuild their lives after the death of a child.

Endorsed by

- Wayne Jacobson, coauthor of *The Shack*
- Darrell Scott, founder of Rachel's Challenge, author, father of Rachel Scott killed in Columbine school shooting (age seventeen)
- Dr. Gloria Horsley, International Grief Counselor, founder of Open to Hope, mother of Scott (age seventeen)
- Several ministry leaders and pastors
- Many bereaved parents

Come Grieve Through Our Eyes: How To Give Comfort And Support To Bereaved Parents By Taking A Glimpse Into Our Hidden Dark World Of Grief

Come Grieve Through Our Eyes gives a clear, truthful message from those who have lost a child, to those who want to know how to be there for these grieving parents. This book opens the door into the world of bereaved parents, enabling the readers to go beyond just condolences and sympathy, but having compassion at a level that will help these devastated parents at their deepest level of need.

From Ring Bearer to Pallbearer: Giving a Voice to Bereaved Siblings and Grandparents

Well-meaning people fail to recognize the depth of the loss of someone who has lost a sibling, making them feel their intense pain isn't valid, and they are not supposed to be hurting so deeply. Grandparents are another group whose grief can get lost in the death of a child. They not only lose their legacy and the relationship with their grandchild, but have to watch their own adult child go through the horrible suffering and trauma at the death of their child. *From Ring Bearer to Pallbearer* shares the thoughts of Laura's youngest son who was a ring bearer for his sister's wedding at age six, and a pallbearer for her casket at age sixteen. The other two brothers share as well, along with all four grandparents. You will see just how different each one is, but they are all valid, just like the grief of every sibling and grandparent is valid.

Triple Crown Transformation: Finding Your Rightful Royal Place in God's Kingdom

Attaining the Triple Crown is a rare accomplishment, whether in horse racing or in baseball. Unfortunately, it is also a rare accomplishment in our lives as a Christian. What is the Triple Crown for a Christian? Laura Diehl believes it is learning 1) how to clarify God's vision for our lives, including being released from our past which keeps us from going forward 2) how to live from a place of authority of being in Christ 3) how to live from a deeper revelation of the identity of the indwelling power of the Holy Spirit. She has dealt with all of these issues through some pretty dark trials; including what many say is the worst thing a person can ever face in this life. Find out what she has learned about vision, authority, and identity in God's Kingdom. *See the Crown...Wear the Crown...Be the Crown!*

(All of Laura's books can be found for sale on www.gpshope.org among other places.)

COMING SOON!
My Grief Journey: Coloring Book for Kids

This new book will have the same drawings as the book you have in your hands, but simplified. It will also be a shorter version, eliminating some of the deeper words. The writing prompt scroll will be blank, with encouragement for the child to draw their own picture. If you want to receive updates and be notified when this book is available, go to **www.crownofgloryministries.org/gpshope-griefjourney-kids/**

Index of Scriptures Used

Old Testament

Genesis 31:49 – Pareavor
Deuteronomy 31:8 – Alone
Psalm 4:4 - Anger
Psalm 23:4 - Comfort
Psalm 30:5 – Resilient
Psalm 56:8 – Tears
Psalm 61:2 – Overwhelmed
Psalm 62:5 – Surrender
Psalm 94:18-19 – Joy
Psalm 118:17-20 – Live
Psalm 147:3 – Healing
Proverbs 3:5-6 – Trust
Proverbs 17:22 – Laughter
Isaiah 41:10 – Shock
Isaiah 43:2 – Numb
Isaiah 49:15-16 – Forgotten
Isaiah 53:3-4 – Sorrow
Isaiah 61:3 – Family
Jeremiah 29:11 – Future
Jeremiah 31:13 – Memories

New Testament

Matthew 11:28-29 - Rest
Matthew 18:21-22 – Forgive
Luke 24:36 - Shattered
John 10:10 - Life
John 15:4-6 - Helpless
John 16:33 - Peace
Romans 8:18 - Pain
Romans 15:13 - Hope
1 Corinthians 14:33 - Confusion
1 Corinthians 15:53-54 - Time
1 Corinthians 15:56-58 - Thankful
2 Corinthians 4:18 - Heaven
Ephesians 3:20 - Thrive
Philippians 3:12 - Journey
Philippians 3:13-14 - Regret
Philippians 4:6-7 - Anxious
1 Thessalonians 2:17 - Longing
2 Timothy 1:9 - Purpose
1 Peter 5:10 - Wounded
2 Peter 3:18 – Grace
1 John 4:19 – Fear
1 John 5:5 – Believe

Made in the USA
San Bernardino, CA
25 June 2016